THE UK NINJA FOODI MAX HEALTH GRILL AND AIR FRYER COOKBOOK

Quick And Delicious Ninja Foodi Grill & Air Fryer Recipes To Grill, Air Fry, Baking, Roasting With European Measurement

MYRTLE SCHAFF

TABLE OF CONTENT

INTRODUCTION

Grilled and satisfyingly Barbequed meals are the heart of any backyard party and/or celebration. They effortlessly liven up the atmosphere and adds an extra layer of jazz to the ambience.

However, as much as we love to make grilled food, preparing them isn't always as easy as one would hope. Several factors come into play when considering an outdoor grill such as the weather, charcoal availability, flame level and of course, skill level of the pit-master. Without having someone experienced in the art of grilling at the helm, the end result might turn out to be a bland and unsatisfying mess. These reasons combined made the hobby of Barbequing and Grilling a very exclusive activity reserved for only the most dedicated individuals.

But not anymore!

Thanks to recent technological advancements in the culinary field, the world of cooking have seen the advent rise of some incredible cooking appliances designed to make the lives of home-chefs a lot easier.

The Ninja Smart Grill XL is an appliance that completely took the world by storm when it first came out, thanks to its unique ability to Grill, Air Fry, and Broil. Dehydrate, Roast, and Bake ingredients all under singlehood!

For those of you who are unaware, the Ninja Smart Grill XL is an indoor electric grill meticulous crafted by the good folks at Ninja Kitchen that has completely revolutionized the grilling scene the features of an outdoor grill and more into a very wholesome and easy to use package.

The Ninja Smart Grill XL has been designed from the ground-up with accessibility kept in mind, ensuring that anyone is able the appliance with ease and prepare the grilled meals of their dreams.

Even though the appliance is designed to be an indoor countertop appliance, it can also be used as an outdoor grill by simply carrying it outside.

The Grill comes packed with a thermometer, crisper basket, kebab skewer set, grill roast rack and a cookbook.

And on top of everything, the Smart Cooking System programmed into the appliance almost guarantees that you will be able to prepared gourmet quality meals with this appliance in no time!

With all of that kept in mind, this particular cookbook has been written to ensure that even the most beginners can pick it up and start effortlessly start grilling with the Ninja Smart Grill XL in no time!

Before you dive into the recipes, feel free to explore the introductory chapter covering all the essential information required to operate the Ninja Smart Grill XL for the first time. Once you are done with the intro, take a gander at the enormous collection of 500 absolutely amazing, handpicked and fool-proof recipes to explore and find your next culinary masterpiece.

Due to the appliance's versatile nature, all of

the recipes are very carefully sub-divided into 9 different categories, so that you can easily find what you are looking for.

So, what are waiting for? Go ahead and download this book and start exploring the amazing world of Grilling with the fantastic Ninja Smart XL Grill!

My cookbook "NINJA FOODI MAX GRILL AND AIR FRYER COOKBOOK" presents 50 yummy, wholesome, and tasty recipes for you. I am very excited to show you my recipes. All recipes are easily prepared with this appliance. I divided recipes into different chapters for your easiness. For example: "Breakfast," "Beef, lamb, and pork recipes," "Chicken and poultry recipes," "Seafood and fish recipes," and "Vegetable recipes." All recipes are prepared for the UK lifestyle (ingredients are available in the UK local market).

Step: 1 – CHOOSE YOUR RECIPES
The first step is choosing your recipes, and in my opinion, this is the best part. Meal prepping does take a little bit of planning.

Step: 2 – PREPARE YOUR INGREDIENTS
In my book, all ingredients are available in UK local market. All components are simple to find. But, keep in mind that buys only fresh ingredients.

Step: 3 – START COOKING
Plug your Ninja foodi MAX health grill and air fryer. Adjust cooking time, temperature, and method. Press the start/stop button to start cooking.

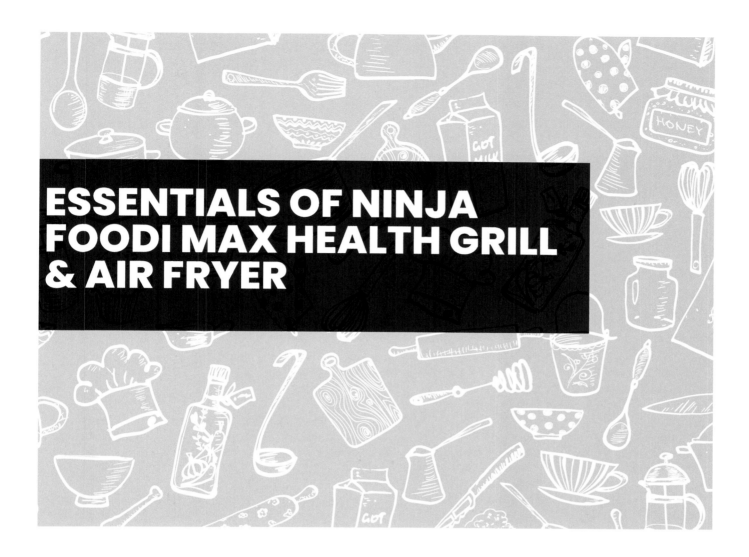

ESSENTIALS OF NINJA FOODI MAX HEALTH GRILL & AIR FRYER

1. WHAT IS THE NINJA SMART XL GRILL

The Ninja Smart XL Grill is possibly one of the most advanced multi-functional electric indoor/ countertop cooking appliances to hit the market to date.

In short, the Ninja Smart XL Grill is a versatile 6 in 1 smokeless countertop grill. But that's not all, this is has an appliance that can Grill, Air Fry, Roast, Bake, Broil and Dehydrate all under singlehood.

It comes packed with a 4 quart-crisper basket that you can use to seamlessly Air Fry/Air Crisp meals. In contrast, a 6-quart cooking basket allows you to cook other meals with ease at a family-sized portion.

Even though you have to grill your meals keeping the lid closed, the food is always in contact with the Grill on only one side, so the grilling mechanism here is similar to an open grill type.

The sleek stainless-steel design of the Ninja Smart XL Grill makes it durable and lighter as well, ensuring that it is the lightest indoor Grill available at the moment.

The Smart XL comes with a 1760 watts power-supply, which is enough to convert frozen foods to mouth-watering char-grilled delights in less than 25 minutes!

On the other hand, the Air Crisp function allows you to prepare guilt-free fried food with minimal oil and minimal effort.

The Ninja Smart XL Grill is bigger than the normal variation but still packs the same punch and can prepare juicily, sizzled and char -flavored meals with ease.

go!

2. WHAT IS IT'S FEATURES AND FUNCTIONS?

The Ninja Grill Smart XL is possibly one of the most versatile and multi-purpose cooking electric outdoor grills.

The most prominent features of the appliance are:

THE SMART COOK SYSTEM

The Ninja Smart XL Grill comes with a revolutionary Smart Cook System with 4 protein settings, 9 customizable doneness level that allows even amateur chefs that allows you to prepare restaurant-quality meals with ease.

XL CAPACITY

The XL version of this appliance has more than 50% grilling capacity than the regular Ninja Grill. It allows you to cook family-sized meals with ease.

AIR FRY CRISP

With the Air Crisp feature, you can Air Fry meals without oil usage and cook healthy meals with ease.

UNIQUE SMOKE CONTROL SYSTEM

Combining the features of the temperature-controlled grill grate, splatter shield and cool air zones, this appliance can reduce smoke while grilling and helps to keep your appliance clean and breezy.

DUAL SENSOR SMART THERMOMETER

The neat dual sense thermometer always monitors the temperature in two places for a more accurate result. This thermometer allows you to multi-task while knowing that your meals are cooked to perfection.

Even though the appliance is a Grill at its heart, there are 5 other functions that you need to know about.

GRILLING

You can seamlessly grill absolutely delicious meals with this function, similar to how you would use an outdoor grill.

This is possibly the most prominent function of this appliance and the one that you will be using the most!

Place the unit into an outlet and power on the Grill.

- Use the grill grate over the cooking pot; choose grill function. The grill function has four default temperature settings: Low at 204 degrees C, Medium at 232 degrees C, High at 260 degrees C, and MAX at 265 degrees C.

- Set the time needed to cook. You may check the grilling cheat sheet that comes with the appliance; it should give you an idea of the time you should use while cooking.

- You must keep checking the food for doneness while cooking to avoid overcooking.

- Once all the required settings are selected, press start and wait for the digital display to show "Add Food."

- The unit will start to preheat and will show progress through the display. It should take about 8 minutes

- If you need to check or flip the food, the cooking timer will automatically pause once you open the lid.

- The screen will show 'Done" once the timer runs out and the meal is complete.

- Turn off the unit and unplug the appliance, leave the hood open to allow the device to cool down faster.

DEHYDRATING

This feature is used to reduce a food's moisture content, and it can be used to prepare dehydrated meals such as jerky or even simple treats for your pets. You should keep in mind that this mode has a slower than usual fan speed and lower temperature, but it still delivers all the flavours.

For dehydrating, follow the steps below:

- Place the first layer of food directly on the cooking pot.

- Add the crisper basket and add one more layer.

- Choose the dehydrate setting and set the timer between 7 to 10 hours. You may check the progress from time to time.

- For cooking frozen foods:

- Choose the medium heat, which is 450° F using the grill option. You may also use the air crisp option if you are cooking fries, vegetables, and other frozen foods.

- Set the time needed for your recipe. Add a few minutes to compensate for the thawing.

- Flip or shake after a few minutes to cook the food evenly.

AIR FRYING/CRISPING

The Air Crisping mode allows you to seamlessly Air Fry or Air Crisp food by circulated superheated air all around it. This mode produces delicious meals without the use of oil.

For Air Crisping, you must place a crisping basket in the pot and close the lid.

- Press the Air Crisp/Air Fry option and then press the start button. The default temperature is set to 390 degrees, and it will preheat for about 3 minutes.

- If you do not need to preheat, simply press the Air Crisp button a second time, and the display will show you "Add Food."

- Put food inside and shake after every 10 minutes. Make sure to use oven mitts or tongs/ with silicone tips while doing this.

BAKING

The baking feature is used for baking meals such as cakes, casseroles and so on.

For baking, remove the grate and use the cooking pot.

Choose the bake setting and set your preferred temperature and time. Pre-heat will take about 3 minutes.

Once done with preheating, you may put the ingredients directly on the cooking pot or use a regular baking tray. An 8-inch baking tray can fit inside as well.

ROASTING

You can use the Ninja Grill Smart XL's roasting feature when you want to finely brown your meats and vegetables. The food's interior will be cooked to perfection while the exterior will get a nice subtle brown.

Remove the Grill from the grates and use the cooking pot that comes with the unit. You may also want to purchase Ninja Kitchen's proprietary roasting rack.

Press the roast option and set the timer between 1 to 4 hours depending on the recipe requirement. Food will be preheated for 3 minutes.

Once done, directly place the meat on the roasting pot and check for doneness while cooking. Enjoy.

BROIL

The broiling feature is perfect for when you need an additional extra browning on the surface of your meal. This is also perfect when you like to caramelize the surface or melt cheese/other toppings.

3. SETTING UP YOUR NINJA SMART XL GRILL

When you are cooking for the first time using the Ninja Grill Smart XL for the first time, it is essential that you wash the detachable cooking parts first, rinse with warm soapy water to remove any oil/debris. Follow the section on washing instructions if you are confused about how to do that.

After that, let it dry and keep it back inside; once you do that, you are ready to cook!

Make sure to position the Grill on a level and secure the surface, leave at least 6-inch space all around it to allow it to breathe and take in air and ensure that the vent and air sockets are not blocked.

Ensure that the splatter guard is installed whenever you are using the Grill.

Once done, simply follow the instructions of the recipes and you are good to do go!

4. PREPARING THE NINJA SMART XL GRILL AND COOKING FOOD FOR THE FIRST TIME

Before starting to cook with your appliance, preheating is a very crucial thing that you should do.

So, turn on the grill and allow it to heat for 8 minutes. Preheating the Grill will ensure that the appliance is ready to accept the meal and cook it properly. While it is preheating, you may do other tasks such as chopping or cutting ingredients required for the meal.

As for the general cooking process,

To start the Ninja Smart XL Grill, simply turn the appliance on and select the cook function that you need, set the timer.

The temperature can be adjusted on the display panel of the Grill.

Once you have picked your desired cooking option and have selected the temperature, the Grill will preheat for a specified amount of time.

The Grill screen will show "Add Food", which is when you insert your meal.

The length of the Grill will vary depending on the temperature that you need.

Higher temperature will take longer to heat up.

5. THE BENEFITS OF USING AN ELECTRIC GRILL

There are countless absolutely excellent benefits of using an indoor electric grill such as the Ninja Smart XL Grill compared to a traditional outdoor grill unit. The most prominent ones are:

GIVES YOUR FULL FREEDOM OVERCOOKING

Even if you have an outdoor grill, there are times when you just might not feel like firing it up, because it requires a significant amount of effort. Several different factors, such as weather, charcoal, and so on need to be kept in check.

With an indoor grill such as the Ninja Smart XL Grill though, you just need electricity, and you can grill any meal that you want with ease.

VERY EASY AND STRAIGHTFORWARD TEMPERATURE CONTROLS

Unlike traditional outdoor Grill that requires very skilled eyes and hands to keep the temperature in check, the Ninja Smart XL Grill is equipped with a great smart thermometer that allows you to regulate the temperature with ease and without any hassle.

With this appliance, your food will never be undercooked or overcooked. All you have to do is just select the temperature and let it do it's magic!

STRAIGHTFORWARD AND SIMPLE AND TO CLEAN

Opposed to outdoor grills, cleaning the Ninja Smart XL Grill is pretty easy to clean. All of this appliance's cooking components are coated with ceramic, making it very easy to clean. The other accessories, such as the Air Crisp basket and heating screen, can be simply washed in a dishwasher.

VERY EASY AND SIMPLE TO USE

Contrary to what some people might say, using the Ninja Smart XL Grill is actually extremely easy. It is possibly one of the most straightforward appliances to use. All you have to do with this is just select the temperature, let the appliance preheat, and wait until you hear a beep.

Once you hear the beep, add food and let it cook on its own!

Once done, the machine will automatically notify you.

While the appliance might be a little bit heavy, you can still easily carry it wherever you want, and it can be used as both an indoor or outdoor appliance.

6. COOKING TIPS AND TRICKS

You may opt to keep the following tips

in your mind for the best cooking experience with the Ninja Grill.

• While smaller than a regular outdoor grill, the Ninja Grill Smart XL is still a relatively heavy machine. Therefore, it is recommended that you did not move the appliance while carrying out its function.

• Although the inbuilt technology is designed to ensure efficient cooking without smoking, you may sometimes experience smoke from time to time. It usually happens because the air mixes with oils and fat. To prevent this, you may use oil with high smoke points such as avocado or grapeseed oil.

• To get the best results, you are recommended that you flip the meal at about half-way between cooking. This will ensure that your meals are grilled to perfection, and you have those awesome grill marks on both sides.

• You should know that the appliance isn't designed to both Grill and air fry simultaneously. Therefore, you mustn't try to do this.

7. UTENSILS AND PANS YOU NEED

Using the appliance on its own is great, but having some additional utensils and accessories would make the experience that much more awesome!

EVO OIL SPRAYER BOTTLE

You may use this pump to spray water, apple juice or anything of that consistency over your meals when needed.

DOT SIMPLE ALARM THERMOMETER

Even though The Ninja Grill Smart XL has a probe thermometer, you should know that there are a number of models that do not. This thermometer will help you keep track of the temperature.

NINJA GRILL ROAST RACK

This rack will give you an additional layer to elevate and roast vegetables/meals.

Ninja XL Grill Combo Crisper Basket

You may use this crisping basket for air crisping meals. It is also awesome for when you want to dehydrate meat/fruits.

Origami Folding Kitchen Carton Wheels

This is an amazing stand for the Ninja Grill Smart XL, and it will free up a good amount of space in your kitchen. You may even roll it to where you need.

KNIFE SHARPENING STONE

If you think about it, you will notice that most of the prep time is spent cutting veggies and meat. Therefore, having a sharp knife is extremely crucial! To that end, try to keep a good quality knife sharpening stone around and sharpen your knives every week or so to keep them in good shape.

CAST IRON PANS

These have been used for centuries and were one of the first modern cooking devices ever! Cast Iron Skillet doesn't wear out and is healthier as no chemicals are used. Asides from that, they also retain heat very well, and you can easily move them between oven and stove. These are simple to clean and wash and doesn't build up rust that easily.

ELECTRIC HAND MIXER

If you have ever had to manually beat an egg using your hand, you know what an arduous task it is! Therefore, you must have a hand mixer nearby as it will save your time and your arm muscles are as well! This is especially helpful when you mix heavy ingredients.

FOOD PROCESSOR

A food processor is extremely crucial to your kitchen and is ideal for blending various foods or processing certain foods together into a sauce or puree.

FOOD SCALE

Suppose you are trying to hit your macronutrient goal. In that case, it is essential to have a kitchen food scale as it will help you to measure any solid or liquid food with the utmost accuracy.

MEASURING SPOON SET

Without a set of measuring spoons, it might be a little tricky to add the proper amount of ingredients. Therefore, you must keep one nearby.

Cutting Boards: Try to get boards made from solid materials such as plastic, glass, rubber or marble! These are mostly corrosion-resistant, and the non-porous surface makes it easier to clean them than wood.

Cold Storage Space (the fridge will suffice): Since the meats must be kept under 40 degrees Fahrenheit, a fridge should be enough.

Knives: Sharp knives should be used to slice the meat accordingly. While using the knife, you should keep the following in mind.

• Always make sure to use a sharp knife

• Never hold a knife under your arm or leave it under a piece of meat

• Always keep your knives within visible distance

• Always keep your knifepoint down

• Always cut down towards the cutting surface and away from your body

• Never allow children to toy with knives unattended

• Wash the knives while cutting

different types of food

8. CARE AND MAINTENANCE TIPS

Despite looking a bit complicated, cleaning the Ninja Smart XL Grill actually pretty easy. Especially if take a methodical and well-defined approach.

It is recommended that you clean up your appliance after every use to keep the appliance crisp and daisy fresh.

The process of safely and effectively cleaning up your appliance is as follows:

• The first step is to allow the appliance to cool down after a cooking session

• Once the appliance is cool, carefully unplug the device from the power outlet

• A good tip will be to keep the hood of your appliance open if you want to let it cool quickly

• The grill gate, splatter shield, crisper basket, cooking pot, cleaning brush and other accessories are completely dishwasher safe, so you can directly put them in your dishwasher/ or clean them by hand

• The thermometer though is not dishwasher safe, and hence you are to clean it manually using a damp cloth

• You may rinse the accessories with additional water and clean them using the provided cleaning brush for an additional polish

• If your cooking basket has baked-on cheese/sauce stuck onto the surface, then you may use the other end of the provided cleaning brush and use it as a scraper to clean them off

• Once done, use a towel or a dryer to dry all of the accessories

• You should keep in mind though that the main unit is not dishwasher safe.

Therefore, you are to take a simple damp cloth and rub the exterior gently. Make sure that you don't use any sort of rasping cleaner as they might damage the surface of the appliance

•   The thermometer is also a very sensitive part, and you should never use any sort of cleaning solution while cleaning it

•   A cotton swab or can of compressed air is suggested to clean the thermometer

Once you are done with the initial cleaning, you may still find some food residue stuck on the surface of the accessories, if that is the case, do the following:

•   If you have any residue stuck on the splatter shield, soak it in warm soapy water solution and clean it up as needed

•   If you have more stubborn dirt, them boil the splatter shield for about 10 minutes for a deep cleaning

If you need to deep clean the thermometer, soak the silicone grip and stainless steel tip in a container full of warm water. Keep in mind that neither the cord nor the jack should be immersed, so make sure that they are not soaked.

The thermometer holder is very sensitive and is to be washed using a damp cloth.

If you follow these instructions properly and to the letter, your appliance will stay in tip-top shape for years to come.

9. SOME COMMON ISSUES THAT YOU MAY FACE WITH THE NINJA SMART XL GRILL

The following are some very common issues and their solutions as presented in the official Ninja Smart Grill XL cookbook. These should help you steer clear some very common problems that new comers seem to face during their early days.

Add Food" appears on the control panel

display.

The unit has completed preheating and it is now time to add your ingredients.

"Shut Lid" appears on the control panel display.

The hood is open and needs to be closed for the selected function to start.

"Plug In" appears on the control panel display.

The thermometer is not plugged into the jack on the right side of the control panel. Plug the thermometer in before proceeding. Press the thermometer in until you hear a click.

"PRBE ERR" appears on the control panel display.

This means the unit timed out before food reached the set internal temperature. As a protection for the unit. it can run for only certain lengths of time at specific temperatures.

WHY IS MY FOOD OVERCOOKED OR UNDERCOOKED EVEN THOUGH I USED THE THERMOMETER?

It is important to insert the thermometer lengthwise into the thickest part of the ingredient to get the most accurate reading. Make sure to allow food to rest for 3-5 minutes to complete cooking. For more information, refer to the Using the Foodi'" Smart Thermometer section.

WHY DOES THE PREHEAT PROGRESS BAR NOT START FRONT THE BEGINNING?

When the unit is warm from previously being used, it will not require the full preheating time.

CAN I CANCEL OR OVERRIDE PREHEATING?

Preheating is highly recommended for best results, but you can skip it by selecting the PREHEAT button after you press the START/

STOP button.

SHOULD I ADD MY INGREDIENTS BEFORE OR AFTER PREHEATING?

For best results, let the unit preheat before adding ingredients.

MY FOOD IS BURNED.

Do not add food until recommended preheat time is complete. For best results, check progress throughout cooking, and remove food when desired level of brownness has been achieved. Remove food immediately after the cook time is complete to avoid overcooking.

WHY DID A CIRCUIT BREAKER TRIP WHILE USING THE UNIT?

The unit uses 1760 watts of power, so it must be plugged into an outlet on a 15-amp circuit breaker. Using an outlet on a 10-amp breaker will cause the breaker to trip. It is also important that the unit be the only appliance plugged into an outlet when in use. To avoid tripping a breaker, make sure the unit is the only appliance plugged into an outlet on a 15-amp breaker.

WHY DOES THE UNIT HAVE A 1-9 STALE FOR THE BEEF PRESET?

Perception of what a specific internal doneness looks like differs from person to person. even restaurant to restaurant. The 1-9 scale provides a wide range of options for each doneness level so you can customize doneness to your liking.

10. COMMON FAQ'S

If this is your first time using the appliance, then you might have some questions in your mind. This section is dedicated to covering some of the common questions that you might have:

IS IT POSSIBLE TO SKIP PREHEATING?

The grill function does not allow for skipping preheat. However, you may press the preheat indicator again after pressing the start button to skip preheating for other functions.

WHAT WOULD BE THE REASON FOR A CIRCUIT BREAKER TRIP?

Because you accidentally plugged the appliance into a circuit breaker less 15 amp.

THE GENERAL RULE OF THUMB TO CONVERT RECIPES TO NINJA SMART XL GRILL?

Select the bake setting, cut down the recipe's temperature by 25 degrees F, and keep checking to ensure that you don't overcook them.

I Got the Ninja Grill XL and every time I preheat it sets off the smoke detector. I spray the grate with Canola oil and the food but it still smokes.

There is no need to spray the grill, you should only ever spray the food, then it will not burn oil and smoke while on preheat.

I'M COOKING STEAKS FOR FIRST TIME, AFTER I'M DONE CAN I AUTOMATICALLY COOK SOME BACON ON THE GRILL THEN SWITCH TO AIR FRYER FOR FRIES?

Sure. I take out the steaks and cook the veggies or whatever else while the steaks rest. I just tent the steaks with some foil.

I HAVE THE XL GRILL 6 IN 1. I WANT TO MAKE A PORK LOIN. IT IS CURRENTLY MARINATING. SHOULD I GRILL IT OR ROAST IT?

Used the probe and the time & temp that the grill told us to & it was perfect!

SEEMS REALLY LOUD, IS EVERYONE ELSE'S THAT WAY?

How close it is to a wall and how are your kitchen acoustics? Depending on your space it might sound loud.

CAN THE SPLATTER SCREEN ON TOP GO IN DISHWASHER?

Yes. So can the pan and grill. Thermometer

can not

IF YOU JUST WANT TO WARM UP LEFTOVERS WOULD YOU USE THE BAKE OPTION AND NOT AIR CRISP?

Air crisp for pizza and day old doughnuts. Just like fresh. Just stick it in there and lift the lid and check on it. Touch it to feel how hot. You can smell the pizza when its done. Don't get hung up on how long. Check frequently at first. You will get do you know about how

long it take.

IS SAFE TO USE DIRECTLY ON THE COUNTERTOP OR WOULD IT BE BEST TO USE A SILICONE MAT OR SOMETHING UNDER IT TO PROTECT THE COUNTERTOP?

The tabletop is fine, it is elevated. They recommend "not" using any type of mat/insulator. Check your manual

BREAKFAST RECIPES

BREAKFAST GRILLED APPLES

 **PREPARATION TIME**
15 MINUTES

 **COOKING TIME**
20 MINUTES

 SERVINGS
4 PERSONS

INGREDIENTS:

- Apples, four
- Butter, 29ml, softened
- Sugar, 14.3g
- Caramel, 59ml
- Pecans, 32g, chopped
- Ground cinnamon, 2.8g

PREPARATIONS:

1. Rinse and clean the apples, cut off the apples, and scoop out the cores with a knife. Cut the holes.
2. Combine the remaining ingredients into the mixing bowl. Stuff the apples with this mixture.
3. Insert grill plate in the cooking pot of Ninja foodi MAX health grill and air fryer and lock the lid. Choose the "grill" option.
4. Adjust the temperature to 176 degrees C. Adjust the cooking time to twenty minutes. Press the start/stop button to start preheating.
5. Place apples onto the grill plate and lock the lid.
6. When done, top with caramel and walnuts.

Nutrition:

CALORIES: 327KCAL, PROTEIN: 3G, CARBOHYDRATE: 44G, FAT: 18G

LEMON BLUEBERRY CRISP

 **PREPARATION TIME**
15 MINUTES

 **COOKING TIME**
30 MINUTES

 SERVINGS
8 PERSONS

INGREDIENTS:

Filling:
- Blueberries, three pints
- Sugar, 64g
- Self rising flour, 32g
- Lemon zest, 5ml, grated
- Lemon juice, 29ml

Topping:
- Gingersnap cookies, 64g, crushed
- Self-rising flour, 64g
- Brown sugar, 64g
- Salt, 0.4g
- Butter, 85g

PREPARATIONS:

1. Combine the filling ingredients into the bowl.
2. Then, mix topping ingredients and add over the filling ingredients.
3. Insert grill plate in the cooking pot of Ninja foodi MAX health grill and air fryer and lock the lid. Choose the "grill" option.
4. Adjust the temperature to 176 degrees C. Adjust the cooking time to thirty to forty-five minutes. Press the start/stop button to start preheating.
5. Place blueberry mixture into the grill plate and lock the lid.
6. When done, remove and serve!

Nutrition:

CALORIES: 434KCAL, PROTEIN: 4G, CARBOHYDRATE: 83G, FAT: 10G

GRILLED BLUEBERRY FRENCH TOAST

 PREPARATION TIME
15 MINUTES

 **COOKING TIME**
30 MINUTES

 SERVINGS
6 PERSONS

INGREDIENTS:

- Cinnamon bread, 1lb
- Milk, 236ml
- Vanilla, 10ml
- Eggs, six
- Cinnamon, 8.4g
- Pecans, 64g, chopped
- Fresh blueberries, 400g
- Maple syrup, 29ml

PREPARATIONS:

1. Place bread slices onto the foil. Bring foil up on sides to make a pan.
2. Whisk the vanilla, cinnamon, syrup, milk, and eggs into the bowl and place over bread. Top with nuts and one cup of blueberries.
3. Insert grill plate in the cooking pot of Ninja foodi MAX health grill and air fryer and lock the lid. Choose the "grill" option.
4. Adjust the temperature to 176 degrees C. Adjust the cooking time to thirty to thirty-five minutes. Press the start/stop button to start preheating.
5. Place foil onto the grill plate. Lock the lid.
6. When done, remove it from the grill.
7. Top with remaining blueberries.

Nutrition:

CALORIES: 499KCAL, PROTEIN: 15G, CARBOHYDRATE: 61G, FAT: 23G

DELICIOUS EGG MUFFINS

 **PREPARATION TIME**
10 MINUTES

 **COOKING TIME**
25 MINUTES

 SERVINGS
6 PERSONS

INGREDIENTS:

- Eggs, 12
- Milk, 118ml
- Salt, 2.8g
- Pepper, 1.4g
- Cheddar cheese, 64g, shredded
- Ham, 64g, diced

PREPARATIONS:

1. Combine pepper, salt, milk, and eggs into the mixing bowl and mix it well. Add ham and cheese and stir well. Place mixture into twelve muffin cups.
2. Insert grill plate in the cooking pot of Ninja foodi MAX health grill and air fryer and lock the lid. Choose the "grill" option.
3. Adjust the temperature to 176 degrees C. Adjust the cooking time to twenty-five to thirty minutes. Press the start/stop button to start preheating.
4. Place muffin cups onto the grill plate. Lock the lid.
5. When done, remove and serve!

Nutrition:

CALORIES: 238KCAL, PROTEIN: 20G, CARBOHYDRATE: 2G, FAT: 16G

MOUTHWATERING BANANA CAKE

PREPARATION TIME
10 MINUTES

COOKING TIME
30 MINUTES

SERVINGS
4 PERSONS

INGREDIENTS:

- Brown sugar, 43g
- Butter, 51ml
- Banana, one, mashed
- Egg, one
- Honey, 29ml
- Self-rising flour, 128g
- Ground cinnamon, 2.8g
- Salt, one pinch

PREPARATIONS:

1. Add butter and sugar into the bowl and beat with an electric mixer until creamy.
2. Mix the honey, egg, and banana in another bowl.
3. Whisk banana mixture to the butter mixture until smooth.
4. Sift salt, cinnamon, and flour into the banana and butter mixture and combine it well. Transfer mixture onto the baking pan.
5. Insert baking pan in the cooking pot of Ninja foodi MAX health grill and air fryer and lock the lid. Choose the "bake" option.
6. Adjust the temperature to 160 degrees C.
   Adjust the cooking time to thirty minutes. Press the start/stop button to start preheating.
7. When done, remove and serve!

Nutrition:

CALORIES: 347KCAL, PROTEIN: 5.2G, CARBOHYDRATE: 56.9G, FAT: 11.8G

CHOCOLATE CHIP COOKIE BITES

 **PREPARATION TIME**
10 MINUTES

 **COOKING TIME**
30 MINUTES

 SERVINGS
17 PERSONS

INGREDIENTS:

- Butter, 118ml, softened
- Brown sugar, 64g
- White sugar, 32g
- Baking soda, 2.8g
- Salt, 2.8g
- Egg, one
- Vanilla extract, 7ml
- Self-rising flour, 241g
- Semisweet chocolate chips, 128g
- Pecans, 113g, chopped and toasted

PREPARATIONS:

1. Add butter into the bowl of an electric mixer at medium to high speed for thirty seconds. Add salt, baking soda, sugar, white sugar, and brown sugar and beat at medium speed for two minutes.
2. Add vanilla extract and egg in it and beat until combined. Add flour and beat as much as possible. Add pecans, chocolate chips, and remaining flour and stir well.
3. Place dough onto the parchment paper and transfer it onto the baking pan.
4. Insert baking pan in the cooking pot of Ninja foodi MAX health grill and air fryer and lock the lid. Choose the "bake" option.
5. Adjust the temperature to 150 degrees C. Adjust the cooking time to eight minutes. Press the start/stop button to start preheating.
6. When done, remove and serve!

Nutrition:

CALORIES: 188KCAL, PROTEIN: 2G, CARBOHYDRATE: 23.6G, FAT: 10.4G

AIR FRYER STRAWBERRY CRISP

 **PREPARATION TIME**
20 MINUTES

 **COOKING TIME**
10 MINUTES

ADDITIONAL TIME
10 MINUTES

 **SERVINGS**
4 PERSONS

INGREDIENTS:

- Fresh strawberries, 320g, diced
- White sugar, 42.5g
- Vanilla extract, 2.4ml
- Salt, 0.4g

Streusel:

- Oats, 32g
- Flour, 32g
- White sugar, 32g
- Butter, 59ml, cubed
- Salt, 0.4g

PREPARATIONS:

1. Add three tbsp sugar and strawberries to the bowl. Let rest for ten to fifteen minutes. Then, add salt and vanilla and stir well. Keep it aside.
2. For the streusel: Mix the salt, butter, sugar, flour, and oat into the bowl and combine with your hands.
3. Insert air fryer basket in the cooking pot of Ninja foodi MAX health grill and air fryer and lock the lid. Choose the "air fry" option.
4. Adjust the temperature to 175 degrees C. Adjust the cooking time to ten to twelve minutes. Press the start/stop button to start preheating.
5. Place strawberry mixture into four ramekins and top with streusel.
6. Place ramekins into the air fryer basket. Lock the lid.
7. When done, remove and serve!

Nutrition:

CALORIES: 280KCAL, PROTEIN: 2.3G, CARBOHYDRATE: 42G, FAT: 12.2G

AIR FRYER BANANA MUFFINS

 **PREPARATION TIME**
5 MINUTES

 **COOKING TIME**
15 MINUTES

 SERVINGS
2-3 PERSONS

INGREDIENTS:

- Banana, two, mashed
- Extra-virgin olive oil, 78ml
- Egg, one
- Brown sugar, 64g
- Vanilla extract, 5ml
- Cinnamon, 5.6g
- Self raising flour, 96g

PREPARATIONS:

1. Add mashed banana, vanilla extract, olive oil, brown sugar, and egg into the mixing bowl and stir to combine. Sprinkle with cinnamon and flour over it. Combine it well.
2. Place mixture into the muffin cups.
3. Insert air fryer basket in the cooking pot of Ninja foodi MAX health grill and air fryer and lock the lid. Choose the "air fry" option.
4. Adjust the temperature to 160 degrees C. Adjust the cooking time to fifteen minutes. Press the start/stop button to start preheating.
5. When done, let cool it.
6. Serve and enjoy!

Nutrition:

CALORIES: 187KCAL, PROTEIN: 2.6G, CARBOHYDRATE: 32.3G, FAT: 5.8G

AIR FRYER MONKEY BREAD

 **PREPARATION TIME**
15 MINUTES

 **COOKING TIME**
15 MINUTES

 SERVINGS
5 PERSONS

INGREDIENTS:

- Cinnamon rolls, 1lb
- Brown sugar, 46g
- Granulated sugar, 46g
- Butter, 44ml, melted
- Ground cinnamon, 1.4g

PREPARATIONS:

1. Cut cinnamon rolls into sixths.
2. Whisk cinnamon, granulated sugar and brown sugar into the bowl.
3. Immerse each cinnamon roll into the melted butter and then roll in the sugar mixture. Place them into the air fryer basket.
4. Insert air fryer basket in the cooking pot of Ninja foodi MAX health grill and air fryer and lock the lid. Choose the "air fry" option.
5. Adjust the temperature to 160 degrees C. Adjust the cooking time to fifteen minutes. Press the start/stop button to start preheating.
6. When done, remove and serve!

Nutrition:

CALORIES: 418KCAL, PROTEIN: 5.3G, CARBOHYDRATE: 61.5G, FAT: 17.7G

GRILLED PEACHES

PREPARATION TIME
5 MINUTES

COOKING TIME
8 MINUTES

SERVINGS
4 PERSONS

INGREDIENTS:

- Ripe peaches, two, sliced in half
- Oil, 29ml
- Cinnamon, 2.8g
- Honey, to drizzle
- Vanilla ice cream, four scoop

PREPARATIONS:

1. Brush the inside of cut peaches with oil.
2. Place peaches onto the grilled plate.
3. Insert grill plate in the cooking pot of Ninja foodi MAX health grill and air fryer and lock the lid. Choose the "grill" option.
4. Adjust the temperature to 160 degrees C. Adjust the cooking time to three to four minutes. Press the start/stop button to start preheating.
5. When done, remove peaches from the grill. Sprinkle with cinnamon and drizzle with honey.
6. Pour vanilla ice cream over peaches.
7. Serve and enjoy!

Nutrition:

CALORIES: 337KCAL, PROTEIN: 5G, CARBOHYDRATE: 35G, FAT: 20G

FISH AND SEAFOOD

GRILLED ONION-BUTTER COD

 **PREPARATION TIME**
10 MINUTES

 **COOKING TIME**
15 MINUTES

 **SERVINGS**
4 PERSONS

Ingredients:

- Unsalted butter, 59ml
- Yellow onion, one, chopped
- White wine, 59ml
- Cod fillets, 0.3lb
- Olive oil, 14ml
- Salt, 2.8g
- Ground black pepper, 2.8g
- Lemon wedges, to serve

Preparations:

1. Add butter into the skillet and heat it. Add onion and cook for one to two minutes. Then, add white wine and simmer for three minutes. When done, remove it from the flame. Let cool it for five minutes.
2. Brush fish fillets with olive oil and season with pepper and salt.
3. Place fish fillets into the crisper basket.
4. Insert crisper basket in the cooking pot of Ninja foodi MAX health grill and air fryer and lock the lid. Choose the "air fryer" option.
5. Adjust the temperature to 160 degrees C. Adjust the cooking time to eight minutes. Press the start/stop button to start preheating.
6. Open the lid and baste the cod with butter sauce. Flip fish and cook for six to seven minutes more.
7. When done, remove it from the appliance.
8. Add sauce over it. Garnish with lemon wedges.

Nutrition:

CALORIES: 308KCAL, PROTEIN: 36G, CARBOHYDRATE: 1G, FAT: 16G

SPECIAL LOBSTER TAILS

PREPARATION TIME
12 MINUTES

COOKING TIME
7 MINUTES

SERVINGS
3-6 PERSONS

Ingredients:

- Lobster tails, six
- Olive oil or melted butter, 59ml
- Fresh lemon juice, 59ml
- Fresh dill, 14.3g
- Salt, 5.6g

Preparations:

1. Split the lobster tail in half and put it onto the cutting board.
2. Cut down through the middle to the shell with a sharp knife.
3. Then, fold the shell back and pat dry it with a paper towel.
4. Mix the salt, dill, lemon juice, butter, or olive oil into the mixing bowl. Then, brush the mixture over the lobster tails.
5. Place lobster tails onto the roasting pan.
6. Insert roasting pan in the cooking pot of Ninja foodi MAX health grill and air fryer and lock the lid. Choose the "roast" option.
7. Adjust the temperature to 160 degrees C. Adjust the cooking time to five to seven minutes. Press the start/stop button to start preheating.
8. When done, remove from the appliance.
9. Serve and enjoy!

Nutrition:

CALORIES: 212KCAL, PROTEIN: 28G, CARBOHYDRATE: 1G, FAT: 10G

GRILLED TUNA STEAKS

 **PREPARATION TIME**
10 MINUTES

 **COOKING TIME**
6 MINUTES

 **SERVINGS**
4 PERSONS

Ingredients:

- Soy sauce, 118ml, low-sodium
- Scallions, 32g, chopped, white and green parts
- Fresh lemon juice, 29ml
- Sesame oil, 5ml
- Ginger, 5.6g, grated
- Tuna steaks, 0.3lb
- Sesame seeds, 64g

Preparations:

1. Mix the ginger, sesame oil, lemon juice, chopped scallions, and soy sauce into the zip-lock bag.
2. Add tuna steaks and coat them with marinade. Let marinate it into the refrigerator for twenty minutes. Seal the bag.
3. Place sesame seeds into the dish. Discard marinade from the steaks and coat with sesame seeds.
4. Place steaks onto the grill plate.
5. Insert grill plate in the cooking pot of Ninja foodi MAX health grill and air fryer and lock the lid. Choose the "grill" option.
6. Adjust the temperature to 200 degrees C. Adjust the cooking time to three minutes. Press the start/stop button to start preheating.
7. Open the lid, flip it and cook for three minutes more.
8. Serve and enjoy!

Nutrition:

CALORIES: 345KCAL, PROTEIN: 55G, CARBOHYDRATE: 7G, FAT: 10G

LIME AND BASIL TILAPIA

 PREPARATION TIME
10 MINUTES

 COOKING TIME
15 MINUTES

 SERVINGS
4 PERSONS

Ingredients:

- Tilapia fillets, four
- Olive oil, 59ml
- Lime juice, 29ml
- Lime, one, zested
- Fresh basil, 14.3g, sliced
- Bourbon, 10ml, optional
- Salt, 5.6g
- Black pepper, to taste

Preparations:

1. Mix the bourbon, fresh basil, lime zest, olive oil, lime juice, pepper, and salt into the bowl.
2. Place tilapia fillets into the zip-lock bag and pour marinade over it. Let seal the bag and marinate it for thirty minutes into the fridge.
3. Insert baking pan in the cooking pot of Ninja foodi MAX health grill and air fryer and lock the lid. Choose the "bake" option.
4. Adjust the temperature to 175 degrees C. Adjust the cooking time to three-five minutes. Press the start/stop button to start preheating.
5. Place fish fillets onto the baking pan and bake for three to five minutes.
6. When done, remove and serve!

Nutrition:

CALORIES: 186KCAL, PROTEIN: 11G, CARBOHYDRATE: 4G, FAT: 15G

CILANTRO LIME FISH HALIBUT

 **PREPARATION TIME**
20 MINUTES

 COOKING TIME
15 MINUTES

 SERVINGS
4 PERSONS

Ingredients:

- Halibut steaks, four
- Fresh cilantro, 96g, chopped
- Butter, 60ml
- Lime juice, 45ml
- Garlic, one clove, minced
- Red pepper flakes, 2.8g
- Salt, 2.8g
- Ground black pepper, 2.8g
- Lime wedges, four to six, to garnish

Preparations:

1. Place halibut onto the baking dish and coat with lime juice. Season with pepper and salt. Keep it aside for twenty minutes.
2. During this, add butter into the saucepan and melt it over medium flame. Then, add garlic and cook for one minute. Add red pepper flakes and cilantro and cook for one minute. Remove from the flame.
3. Insert baking pan in the cooking pot of Ninja foodi MAX health grill and air fryer and lock the lid. Choose the "bake" option.
4. Adjust the temperature to 175 degrees C. Adjust the cooking time to five-seven minutes. Press the start/stop button to start preheating.
5. Open the lid and baste with butter sauce.
6. Garnish with lime wedges.

Nutrition:

CALORIES: 557KCAL, PROTEIN: 76G, CARBOHYDRATE: 27G, FAT: 17G

BLACKENED RED SNAPPER

 **PREPARATION TIME**
10 MINUTES

 **COOKING TIME**
12 MINUTES

 **SERVINGS**
4 PERSONS

Ingredients:

- Paprika, 5.6g
- Cayenne, 1.4g
- Salt, 5.6g
- Garlic salt, 2.8g
- Onion salt, 2.8g
- Dried thyme, 5.6g
- Dried oregano, 5.6g
- Black pepper, 2.8g
- Red snapper fillets, two, halved
- Lemon juice, 29ml
- Butter, 118ml
- Parsley, 14g, minced

Preparations:

1. Combine the pepper, oregano, thyme, garlic salt, onion salt, salt, cayenne, and paprika into the bowl. Sprinkle the seasoning over each side of the red snapper.
2. Insert roasting pan in the cooking pot of Ninja foodi MAX health grill and air fryer and lock the lid. Choose the "roast" option.
3. Adjust the temperature to 200 degrees C. Adjust the cooking time to five-six minutes. Press the start/stop button to start preheating.
4. Meanwhile, add lemon juice into the saucepan and heat it. Then, add butter and cook it. Remove from the flame.
5. When the red snapper is cooked, remove it from the appliance.
6. Top with lemon butter and butter mixture.
7. Serve and enjoy!

Nutrition:

CALORIES: 319KCAL, PROTEIN: 23G, CARBOHYDRATE: 2G, FAT: 25G

GRILLED GINGER-LIME SWORDFISH

 **PREPARATION TIME**
15 MINUTES

 COOKING TIME
10 MINUTES

 SERVINGS
2 PERSONS

Ingredients:

- Swordfish steaks, six ounces
- Honey, 44ml
- Soy sauce, 44ml
- Vegetable oil, 14ml
- Garlic, one to two cloves, minced
- Fresh ginger, 14.3g, grated
- Lime zest, 5ml
- Lime, one, juiced
- White pepper, 1.4g

Preparations:

1. Place fish into the bowl. Mix the marinade ingredients in another bowl. Pour marinade over fish and coat it well. Cover the dish with plastic wrap. Put it into the refrigerator for 1 and ½ hours.
2. Insert grill plate in the cooking pot of Ninja foodi MAX health grill and air fryer and lock the lid. Choose the "grill" option.
3. Adjust the temperature to 175 degrees C. Adjust the cooking time to three-four minutes. Press the start/stop button to start preheating.
4. Open the lid, flip and cook for five minutes more.
5. When done, remove from the grill.
6. Serve and enjoy!

Nutrition:

CALORIES: 518KCAL, PROTEIN: 7G, CARBOHYDRATE: 54G, FAT: 14G

HONEY-DIJON ARCTIC CHAR

 PREPARATION TIME
10 MINUTES

 COOKING TIME
10 MINUTES

 SERVINGS
4 PERSONS

Ingredients:

- Arctic char fillets, four, 1 1/2 inches thick
- Dijon mustard, 120ml
- Honey, 120ml
- Olive oil, 30ml
- Garlic, three cloves, minced
- Fresh thyme, 10g
- Sea salt, 5.6g
- White pepper, 2.8g
- Juice of lemon, one

Preparations:

1. Rinse fish under cold water and pat dry with a paper towel.
2. Place fish onto the baking dish. Mix the white pepper, salt, lemon juice, thyme, garlic, oil, honey, and mustard into a small bowl. Coat fish fillets with mixture. Cover the dish with plastic wrap and put it into the fridge for thirty to forty minutes.
3. Place fish fillets onto the baking pan.
4. Insert baking pan in the cooking pot of Ninja foodi MAX health grill and air fryer and lock the lid. Choose the "bake" option.
5. Adjust the temperature to 175 degrees C. Adjust the cooking time to five minutes. Press the start/stop button to start preheating.
6. Open the lid and cook for five minutes more.
7. When done, serve and enjoy!

Nutrition:

CALORIES: 541KCAL, PROTEIN: 63G, CARBOHYDRATE: 54G, FAT: 17G

LEMON AND BALSAMIC SOLE FILLETS

 PREPARATION TIME
15 MINUTES

 COOKING TIME
10 MINUTES

 SERVINGS
4 PERSONS

Ingredients:

- Sole fillet, 1 ¼ lbs, and 1/8-inch to ¼-inch thick pieces
- Balsamic vinegar, 59ml
- Fresh lemon juice, 59ml
- Dry mustard, 5.6g
- Yellow onion, one, chopped
- Fresh parsley, 10g, chopped
- Lemon, one, cut into slices
- Salt and ground black pepper, to taste

Preparations:

1. Rinse and pat dry the sole fillets with a paper towel. Place onto the dish.
2. Mix the chopped parsley, onion, mustard, lemon juice, and balsamic vinegar into the bowl. Pour over sole fish and let marinate for twenty to thirty minutes into the fridge.
3. Discard marinade and place fish onto the roasting pan.
4. Insert roasting pan in the cooking pot of Ninja foodi MAX health grill and air fryer and lock the lid. Choose the "roast" option.
5. Adjust the temperature to 200 degrees C. Adjust the cooking time to four to six minutes.
   Press the start/stop button to start preheating.
6. When cooked, season with pepper and salt.
7. Garnish with lemon slices.

Nutrition:

CALORIES: 150KCAL, PROTEIN: 22G, CARBOHYDRATE:6G, FAT: 4G

GRILLED BLACKENED TILAPIA

 **PREPARATION TIME**
10 MINUTES

 **COOKING TIME**
5 MINUTES

 SERVINGS
4 PERSONS

Ingredients:

- Tilapia, 1lb
- Butter, 14ml

Blackening Rub:

- Paprika, 42g
- Salt, 14.3g
- Onion powder, 14.3g
- Black pepper, 5.6g
- Dry thyme, 5.6g
- Dry oregano, 5.6g
- Garlic powder, 2.8g
- Cayenne pepper, 1.4g to 5.6g

Preparations:

1. Mix blackened rub ingredients into the bowl.
2. Rinse and pat dry the tilapia and rub the mixture over it.
3. Microwave butter and melt it. Brush tilapia fillets with melted butter.
4. Insert grill plate in the cooking pot of Ninja foodi MAX health grill and air fryer and lock the lid. Choose the "grill" option.
5. Adjust the temperature to 200 degrees C. Adjust the cooking time to five minutes. Press the start/stop button to start preheating.
6. Place coated tilapia onto the grill plate. Lock the lid.
7. When done, remove and serve!

Nutrition:

CALORIES: 154KCAL, PROTEIN: 23G, CARBOHYDRATE: 4G, FAT: 5G

BEEF LAMB AND PORK

YUMMY BEEF SATAY

PREPARATION TIME
15 MINUTES

COOKING TIME
10 MINUTES

SERVINGS
4 PERSONS

INGREDIENTS:

- Ginger root, 14.3g, grated
- Garlic, four cloves, crushed
- Onion, 29ml, minced
- Brown sugar, 32g
- Fish sauce, 59ml
- Vegetable oil, 29ml
- Soy sauce, 29ml
- Ground coriander, 28.3g
- Ground cumin, 14.3g
- Ground turmeric, 2.8g
- Cayenne pepper, 0.4g
- Beef top sirloin, 2lbs, trimmed

PREPARATIONS:

1. Add cayenne pepper, turmeric, cumin, coriander, soy sauce, vegetable oil, fish sauce, brown sugar, onion, garlic, and ginger into the mixing bowl. Whisk to combine.
2. Cut beef sirloin into strips and combine into the marinade. Cover the bowl with plastic wrap. Let marinate it for two to four hours into the refrigerator. Discard marinade and thread meat onto the skewers.
3. Plug probe in the Ninja foodi MAX health grill and air fryer and close the lid. Choose the "roast" option. Press "preset" and "beef." Adjust temperature to 200 degrees C. Adjust cooking time for ten minutes.
4. Press the start/stop button to start preheating.
5. When preheated, insert the probe into the center of the beef skewers.
6. Place beef skewers onto the roasting pan and close the lid.
7. When done, let cool it for two minutes.
8. Serve and enjoy!

Nutrition:

CALORIES: 484KCAL, PROTEIN: 40.1G, CARBOHYDRATE: 19.2G, FAT: 26.8G

GRILLED DELMONICO STEAKS

 PREPARATION TIME
10 MINUTES

 COOKING TIME
20 MINUTES

 SERVINGS
4 PERSONS

INGREDIENTS:

- Olive oil, 118ml
- Worcestershire sauce, 59ml
- Soy sauce, 88ml
- Garlic, 32g, minced
- Onion, half, chopped
- Salt, 28.3g
- Pepper, 14.3g
- Rosemary, 14.3g, crushed
- Steak seasoning, 42g
- Steak sauce, 44ml
- Delmonico or rib-eye steaks, 0.6lb

PREPARATIONS:

1. Mix the steak sauce, steak seasoning, rosemary, pepper, salt, onion, garlic, soy sauce, Worcestershire sauce, and olive oil into the food processor and process until combined.
2. Cut steak with a fork and place it into the shallow dish. Pour marinade over it and marinate it for three hours.
3. Insert grill plate in the cooking pot of Ninja foodi MAX health grill and air fryer and lock the lid. Choose the "grill" option.
4. Adjust the temperature to 160 degrees C. Adjust the cooking time to ten minutes. Press the start/stop button to start preheating.
5. Place steaks onto the grill plate. Lock the lid.
6. When done, remove and serve!

Nutrition:

CALORIES: 676KCAL, PROTEIN: 33.7G, CARBOHYDRATE: 14.8G, FAT: 53.6G

LAMB KABOBS

 **PREPARATION TIME**
20 MINUTES

 **COOKING TIME**
12 MINUTES

 **SERVINGS**
20 PERSONS

INGREDIENTS:

- Lamb shoulder, 5lbs, cut into 1 inch pieces, boneless
- Dijon mustard, 88ml
- White wine vinegar, 59ml
- Extra-virgin olive oil, 59ml
- Salt, 2.8g
- Black pepper, 2.8g
- Rosemary, 2.8g, chopped
- Dried sage, 2.8g, crumbled
- Garlic, four cloves, chopped
- Green bell peppers, four, cut into large chunks
- Whole fresh mushrooms, 283g
- Pineapple chunks, 453g, drained with juice reserved
- Cherry tomatoes, one pint
- Onions, four, quartered
- Maraschino cherries, 283g, drained and juice reserved
- Melted butter, 78ml

PREPARATIONS:

1. Place lamb into the bowl.
2. Add garlic, sage, rosemary, pepper, salt, olive oil, vinegar, and mustard in another bowl. Place this mixture over the lamb and combine it well. Cover with plastic wrap. Refrigerate it overnight.
3. Thread the vegetables, fruits, and lamb onto the skewers.
4. Add melted butter, juice of cherries, and pineapple in a small bowl to make a basting sauce.
5. Insert roasting pan in the cooking pot of Ninja foodi MAX health grill and air fryer and lock the lid. Choose the "roast" option.
6. Adjust the temperature to 200 degrees C. Adjust the cooking time to twelve minutes. Press the start/stop button to start preheating.
7. Open the lid and brush with butter sauce.
8. When done, remove and serve!

Nutrition:

CALORIES: 406KCAL, PROTEIN: 20G, CARBOHYDRATE: 13.2G, FAT: 30.3G

GRILLED LAMB BURGERS

 PREPARATION TIME
25 MINUTES

 COOKING TIME
10 MINUTES

 SERVINGS
5 PERSONS

INGREDIENTS:

- Ground lamb, 1 ¼lbs
- Egg, one
- Dried oregano, 5.6g
- Dry sherry, 5.6g
- White wine vinegar, 5ml
- Red pepper flakes, 2.8g, crushed
- Garlic, four cloves, minced
- Green onions, 64g, chopped
- Fresh mint, 14.3g, chopped
- Fresh cilantro, 28.3g, chopped
- Dry bread crumbs, 28.3g
- Salt, 0.4g
- Ground black pepper, 1.4g
- Hamburger buns, five rolls

PREPARATIONS:

1. Combine the pepper, salt, breadcrumbs, cilantro, mint, green onions, garlic, red pepper flakes, vinegar, sherry, oregano, egg, and lamb into the mixing bowl. Make five patties from this mixture.
2. Insert grill plate in the cooking pot of Ninja foodi MAX health grill and air fryer and lock the lid. Choose the "grill" option.
3. Adjust the temperature to 160 degrees C. Adjust the cooking time to eight minutes. Press the start/stop button to start preheating.
4. Place patties onto the grill plate and lock the lid.
5. When done, remove from the grill.
6. Serve in hamburgers buns with lettuce leaves, tomatoes, onions, and mayonnaise.

Nutrition:

CALORIES: 376KCAL, PROTEIN: 25.5G, CARBOHYDRATE: 25.4G, FAT: 18G

SPICY LAMB PATTIES

PREPARATION TIME
10 MINUTES

COOKING TIME
15 MINUTES

SERVINGS
4 PERSONS

INGREDIENTS:

- Ground lamb, 1lb
- Green onions, three, minced
- Garlic, four cloves, minced
- Curry powder, 14.3g
- Ground cumin, 5.6g
- Dried red pepper flakes, 1.4g
- Salt and pepper, to taste

PREPARATIONS:

1. Combine pepper, salt, red pepper, cumin, curry powder, garlic, lamb, and green onions into the bowl. Make four patties from this mixture.
2. Insert grill plate in the cooking pot of Ninja foodi MAX health grill and air fryer and lock the lid. Choose the "grill" option.
3. Adjust the temperature to 200 degrees C. Adjust the cooking time to five minutes. Press the start/stop button to start preheating.
4. Place patties onto the grill plate and lock the lid.
5. When done, remove and serve with mayonnaise.

Nutrition:

CALORIES: 237KCAL, PROTEIN: 20.1G, CARBOHYDRATE: 3.1G, FAT: 15.8G

ROASTED MOJO BEEF

PREPARATION TIME
10 MINUTES

COOKING TIME
8 MINUTES

SERVINGS
4 PERSONS

INGREDIENTS:

- Beef skirt steak, 2lbs
- Orange, one, juiced
- Limes, three, juiced
- Olive oil, 59ml
- Garlic, six cloves, minced
- Salt, 14.3ml
- Ground cumin, 8.4g
- Ground black pepper, 5.6g
- Dried oregano, 2.8g
- Cayenne pepper, 2.8g
- Onion, half, thinly sliced
- Coriander, 64g, chopped
- Salt, 5.6g
- Lime wedges, to serve

PREPARATIONS:

1. Cut skirt steaks into three to four pieces and place them into the mixing bowl.
2. Whisk the cayenne pepper, oregano, pepper, cumin, salt, garlic, olive oil, lime juice, and orange juice into the bowl. Add skirt steak pieces into the marinade and coat it well. Then, add sliced onions and toss to combine.
3. Transfer it to the zip-lock bag and seal it. Place it into the fridge for two to three hours.
4. Insert roasting pan in the cooking pot of Ninja foodi MAX health grill and air fryer and lock the lid. Choose the "roast" option.
5. Adjust the temperature to 175 degrees C. Adjust the cooking time to three to five minutes. Press the start/stop button to start preheating.
6. Place the beef onto the roasting pan and lock the lid.
7. When done, transfer it to the dish.
8. Cut it into slices add juice over it.
9. Drizzle with olive oil—season with salt. Garnish with fresh coriander. Serve with lime wedges.

Nutrition:

CALORIES: 382KCAL, PROTEIN: 29.1G, CARBOHYDRATE: 16G, FAT: 23.2G

HAM AND PINEAPPLE KABOBS

PREPARATION TIME
15 MINUTES

COOKING TIME
8 MINUTES

SERVINGS
4 PERSONS

INGREDIENTS:

- Brown sugar, 42g
- White vinegar, 28g
- Vegetable oil, 14ml
- Prepared mustard, 5.6g
- Ham, ¾ lb, cooked, cut into 1 inch cubes
- Pineapple chunks, 425g, drained

PREPARATIONS:

1. Combine mustard, vegetable oil, vinegar, and brown sugar into the bowl.
2. Thread ham and pineapple chunks onto the skewers.
3. Insert roasting pan in the cooking pot of Ninja foodi MAX health grill and air fryer and lock the lid. Choose the "roast" option.
4. Adjust the temperature to 200 degrees C. Adjust the cooking time to six to eight minutes. Press the start/stop button to start preheating.
5. Place skewers onto the roasting pan and lock the lid.
6. When done, remove and serve!

Nutrition:

CALORIES: 342KCAL, PROTEIN: 16.2G, CARBOHYDRATE: 26.8G, FAT: 19.3G

BABY BACK RIBS

 **PREPARATION TIME**
15 MINUTES

 COOKING TIME
1 HOUR

 SERVINGS
4 PERSONS

INGREDIENTS:

- Mesquite chips, 128g, soaked
- Slab baby back pork ribs, 2lbs
- Salt, 5.6g
- Ground pepper, 5.6g
- Hungarian paprika, 5.6g
- Red chili powder, 5.6g
- Ground thyme, 2.8g
- Barbeque sauce, 236ml

PREPARATIONS:

1. Prepare the membrane from the ribs.
2. Mix the thyme, red chili powder, paprika, pepper, and salt into the bowl and rub over the ribs. Cut slab of ribs in half.
3. Insert grill plate in the cooking pot of Ninja foodi MAX health grill and air fryer and lock the lid. Choose the "grill" option.
4. Adjust the temperature to 200 degrees C. Adjust the cooking time to twenty minutes. Press the start/stop button to start preheating.
5. Place skewers onto the grill plate and lock the lid.
6. Open the lid, baste with BBQ sauce. Lock the lid and cook for thirty minutes more.
7. When done, remove and serve!

Nutrition:

CALORIES: 465KCAL, PROTEIN: 24.2G, CARBOHYDRATE: 23.5G, FAT: 29.7G

STEAK AND NOODLE BOWL

PREPARATION TIME
15 MINUTES

COOKING TIME
44 MINUTES

SERVINGS
4 PERSONS

INGREDIENTS:

- Soy sauce, 118ml, low-sodium
- Vegetable oil, 78ml
- Brown sugar, 43g
- Ginger, 14.3g, minced
- Garlic powder, 2.8g
- Flank steak, 2lbs
- dried Noodles, 283g
- Snow peas, 170g
- Broccoli florets, 128g
- Sweet wine, 14ml

PREPARATIONS:

1. Whisk garlic powder, ginger, brown sugar, vegetable oil, soy sauce into the bowl.
2. Cut flank steak using a big fork. Add it to the bowl and cover it with plastic wrap. Let marinate it into the fridge for four hours.
3. Add salt and water into the pot and boil it. Add dried noodles in the boiled water until tender, for thirteen to fourteen minutes. Then, drain it.
4. Remove steak from marinade and cook for two minutes per side.
5. Insert roasting pan in the cooking pot of Ninja foodi MAX health grill and air fryer and lock the lid. Choose the "roast" option.
6. Adjust the temperature to 150 degrees C. Adjust the cooking time to ten minutes per side. Press the start/stop button to start preheating.
7. Place skewers onto the roasting pan and lock the lid.
8. Cut steaks thinly.
9. Add sweet wine, broccoli florets, snow peas, and remaining marinade into the skillet and mix it well. Let cook over medium-high flame for two minutes. Add drained noodles in it and combine it again.
10. Divide noodle mixture between bowls.
11. Top with steak slices.

Nutrition:

CALORIES: 660KCAL, PROTEIN: 35.9G, CARBOHYDRATE: 61.6G, FAT: 28.5G

GRILLED BACON SUSHI ROLL

 PREPARATION TIME
15 MINUTES

 COOKING TIME
35 MINUTES

 SERVINGS
4 PERSONS

INGREDIENTS:

- Bacon, six, thick slices
- Lean ground beef, half pound
- Barbeque spice rub, 14.3g
- Prosciutto, four, thinly slices
- Jalapeno peppers, two, sliced into long strips
- Pepper Jack cheese, two sticks
- Barbeque sauce, 29ml
- French-fried onions, 128g

PREPARATIONS:

1. Place bacon slices on the sushi mat.
2. Combine spice rub and ground beef into the bowl.
3. Spread in a thin layer over bacon. Top with prosciutto. Add jalapeno strips and add over cheese sticks. Roll up.
4. Insert grill plate in the cooking pot of Ninja foodi MAX health grill and air fryer and lock the lid. Choose the "grill" option.
5. Adjust the temperature to 175 degrees C. Adjust the cooking time to twenty-five minutes per side. Press the start/stop button to start preheating.
6. Place rolls onto the grill plate and lock the lid.
7. Open the lid and baste with BBQ sauce. Cook for five minutes.
8. Baste with remaining BBQ sauce and grill for five minutes more.
9. Serve and enjoy!

Nutrition:

CALORIES: 660KCAL, PROTEIN: 21.1G, CARBOHYDRATE: 28.2G, FAT: 49.4G

POULTRY

GRILLED CHICKEN SHAWARMA

 **PREPARATION TIME**
30 MINUTES

 **COOKING TIME**
25 MINUTES

 **SERVINGS**
6 PERSONS

Ingredients:

- Chicken thighs, 2lbs, boneless and skinless

Shawarma Marinade:
- Ground cumin, 28.3g
- Ground coriander, 28.3
- Garlic, eight cloves, minced
- Salt, 8.4g
- Olive oil, 88ml
- Cayenne pepper, 1.4g
- Turmeric, 8.4g
- Ground ginger, 4.2g
- Ground black pepper, 4.2g
- Allspice, 8.4g

White sauce:
- Juice of lemon, one
- Garlic, twelve to fifteen, cloves
- Salt, 1.9g
- Extra-virgin olive oil, or grape seed oil, 236ml

Preparations:

1. Add all marinade ingredients into the food processor and blend until combine.
2. Rub this mixture all over the chicken and let rest for twenty minutes.
3. Cut chicken into the cubes and marinate for skewers. Place onto the grill plate.
4. Insert grill plate in the cooking pot of Ninja foodi MAX health grill and air fryer and lock the lid. Choose the "grill" option.
5. Adjust the temperature to 170 degrees C. Adjust the cooking time to eight minutes. Press the start/stop button to start preheating.

To prepare the white sauce:

1. Add salt, lemon, and garlic into the food processor and blend until smooth. Add olive oil and blend again.
2. Pour sauce over shawarma chicken.

Nutrition:

CALORIES: 314KCAL, PROTEIN: 32.3G, CARBOHYDRATE: 4.8G, FAT: 18.5G

TURKEY BURGERS WITH SLAW

 PREPARATION TIME
30 MINUTES

 COOKING TIME
15 MINUTES

 SERVINGS
3-4 PERSONS

Ingredients:

Turkey Burger:
- Ground turkey, 1lb
- Shallot, 42g, diced
- Ginger, 8.4g, grated
- Garlic, two cloves, minced
- Lemongrass, 14.3g, chopped
- Basil, 28.3g, chopped
- Lime zest, 5ml
- Scallion, one, chopped
- Jalapeno, half, seeded and chopped
- Fish sauce, 14ml
- Sugar, 5.6g
- White pepper,1.4g, optional

Crunchy Asian Slaw:
- Carrots, 128g, grated
- Cabbage, 128g, shredded
- Scallion, one, thinly sliced
- Lime juice or rice wine vinegar, two tbsp
- Extra-virgin olive oil, 14ml
- Sugar, 5.6g
- Salt and pepper, 1.4g

Spicy Aioli:
- Tartar sauce, 59ml
- Sriracha or chili garlic sauce, 14ml

Preparations:

1. Mix all burger ingredients into the bowl and combine it well.
2. Shape into three burgers and place them into the refrigerator.
3. Toss the slaw ingredients into the bowl.
4. Combine the spicy aioli ingredients into the bowl.
5. Place patties onto the grilled plate.
6. Insert grill plate in the cooking pot of Ninja foodi MAX health grill and air fryer and lock the lid. Choose the "grill" option.
7. Adjust the temperature to 175 degrees C. Adjust the cooking time to four to five minutes. Press the start/stop button to start preheating.
8. Grill the buns and spread aioli onto the bun and top with patty. Top with slaw and aioli and top with another bun.
9. Serve and enjoy!

Nutrition:

CALORIES: 526KCAL, PROTEIN: 33G, CARBOHYDRATE: 41G, FAT: 26G

GRILLED CHICKEN WITH SALSA VERDE

 PREPARATION TIME
20 MINUTES

 COOKING TIME
25 MINUTES

 SERVINGS
4 PERSONS

Ingredients:

- Chicken, four to six pieces
- Pepper and salt, to taste

Salsa Verde:
- Parsley, 128g
- Garlic, two cloves
- Lemon juice, 29ml
- Lemon zest, 10ml
- Capers, 28.3g
- Caper juice, 14ml
- Anchovy, one
- Extra-virgin olive oil, 78ml
- Salt and pepper, 1.4g

Tuscan Tomato Salad:
- Heirloom tomatoes, 2lbs
- Extra-virgin olive oil, 29ml
- Balsamic vinegar, 29ml
- Salt and pepper to taste
- Herbs, optional

Preparations:

1. Season chicken with pepper and salt.
2. Place chicken onto the grilled plate.
3. Insert grill plate in the cooking pot of Ninja foodi MAX health grill and air fryer and lock the lid. Choose the "grill" option.
4. Adjust the temperature to 175 degrees C. Adjust the cooking time to ten to fifteen minutes. Press the start/stop button to start preheating.

To prepare salsa Verde:
1. Add all ingredients into the food processor and blend fifteen times until chopped. Transfer it to the bowl. Keep it aside.

To prepare tomato salad:
1. Cut tomatoes and place them onto the plate.
2. Top with pepper, salt, balsamic vinegar, and olive oil.
3. Spread herbs.
4. When the chicken has been grilled, serve with tomato salad and pour salsa Verde over chicken.

Nutrition:

CALORIES: 416KCAL, PROTEIN: 25.8G, CARBOHYDRATE: 3.8G, FAT: 26.8G

GRILLED CHICKEN SOUVLAKI WITH CAULIFLOWER RICE

 PREPARATION TIME
20 MINUTES

 COOKING TIME
20 MINUTES

 SERVINGS
2-3 PERSONS

Ingredients:

Marinade:
- Garlic, four cloves
- Zest lemon, one
- Lemon juice, 14ml
- Olive oil, 14ml
- Oregano, 8.4g, chopped
- Salt, 5.6g
- Black pepper, 2.8g
- Cayenne, one pinch
- Chicken breast, 1lb, boneless

Cucumber yogurt sauce:
- Plain yogurt, 177ml
- Garlic – one clove, minced
- Olive oil, 14ml
- Lemon juice, 14ml
- Salt, 1.4g
- Cucumber, 128g, diced
- Parsley or mint, 28g
- Chili flakes or pepper, to taste

Cauliflower Rice:
- Olive oil, 14ml
- Shallot, one
- Garlic, two cloves, minced
- Cauliflower rice, 384g
- Pepper, salt, and cayenne, to taste
- Lemon zest, fresh herbs, optional

Optional ingredients:
- Cucumber, 256g, diced
- Tomatoes – 256g, sliced in half or diced
- Avocado, one, sliced
- Mint, few leaves

Preparations:

1. Add marinade ingredients into the bowl and stir well.
2. Add chicken and toss to combine. Let rest it at room temperature.

To prepare cucumber yogurt sauce:
1. Add all ingredients into the bowl and stir well.

To prepare cauliflower rice:
1. Add oil into the skillet and cook over medium-high flame.
2. Add shallot and cook for two minutes.
3. Reduce the heat to medium. Then, add garlic and cook for one minute more. Add cauliflower rice and cook for two minutes.
4. Reduce the heat to medium-low.
5. Insert grill plate in the cooking pot of Ninja foodi MAX health grill and air fryer and lock the lid. Choose the "grill" option.
6. Adjust the temperature to 200 degrees C. Adjust the cooking time to five minutes. Press the start/stop button to start preheating.
7. Place chicken onto the grill plate and lock the lid.
8. Return to cauliflower rice, cook for few minutes. Then, add seasoning.
9. When done, remove from the flame.
10. When chicken is done, remove it from the grill.

Assemble:
1. Add cauliflower rice into the bowl. Pour cucumber yogurt sauce over it. Surround with chicken. Sprinkle with fresh herbs, olive oil, and salt, avocado, tomato, and cucumber.

Nutrition:

CALORIES: 168KCAL, PROTEIN: 22G, CARBOHYDRATE: 1.8G, FAT: 7.7G

GRILLED HULI HULI CHICKEN

PREPARATION TIME
5 MINUTES

COOKING TIME
25 MINUTES

SERVINGS
4 PERSONS

Ingredients:

- Brown sugar, 64g
- Ketchup, 118ml
- Soy sauce, 118ml
- Rice vinegar, 78ml
- Ginger, one knob, minced
- Garlic, three cloves, minced
- Chicken thighs or breasts, 4lbs
- Cilantro, few sprigs, chopped
- Green onions, chopped

Preparations:

1. To prepare the marinade: Whisk the garlic, ginger, rice vinegar, soy sauce, ketchup, and brown sugar into the plastic bag. Place chicken into the marinade and let marinate it for two hours.
2. Insert grill plate in the cooking pot of Ninja foodi MAX health grill and air fryer and lock the lid. Choose the "grill" option.
3. Adjust the temperature to 200 degrees C. Adjust the cooking time to twenty to twenty-five minutes. Press the start/stop button to start preheating.
4. Place chicken onto the grill plate and lock the lid.
5. When done, top with green onions and chopped cilantro.

Nutrition:

CALORIES: 627KCAL, PROTEIN: 44G, CARBOHYDRATE: 37G, FAT: 33G

GRILLED BBQ CHICKEN PIZZA

 PREPARATION TIME
30 MINUTES

 COOKING TIME
10 MINUTES

 SERVINGS
8 PERSONS

Ingredients:

- Pizza dough, 1lb
- Flour, for dusting
- Olive oil, for brushing
- BBQ sauce, 118ml
- Mozzarella cheese, 160g, shredded
- Tomato, 43g, thinly sliced
- Green bell peppers, 43g, thinly sliced
- Red onion, 43g, thickly sliced
- Corn, 64g, fresh
- Bacon, two sliced, cooked and diced
- Chicken breast, 0.3lb, cooked and thickly sliced
- Green onions, 1.4g, thinly sliced

Preparations:

1. Place pizza dough onto the floured piece of parchment paper.
2. Brush the top of the dough with olive oil.
3. Insert grill plate in the cooking pot of Ninja foodi MAX health grill and air fryer and lock the lid. Choose the "grill" option.
4. Adjust the temperature to 160 degrees C. Adjust the cooking time to four minutes. Press the start/stop button to start preheating.
5. Place pizza dough onto the grill plate and lock the lid.
6. Open the lid, flip the dough and place cooked chicken, bacon, corn, onion, bell pepper, tomato, mozzarella cheese, and BBQ sauce over it. Lock the lid and cook for four to five minutes until cheese is melted.
7. When done, remove pizza from the grill.
8. Top with BBQ sauce and green onions.
9. Cut into eight slices.
10. Serve and enjoy!

Nutrition:

CALORIES: 391KCAL, PROTEIN: 26G, CARBOHYDRATE: 36G, FIBER: 3G

BBQ CHICKEN SANDWICHES WITH COLESLAW

 PREPARATION TIME
30 MINUTES

 COOKING TIME
15 MINUTES

 SERVINGS
4 PERSONS

Ingredients:

Chicken Sandwiches:
- Chicken breast, 2lbs, skinless
- Dark brown sugar, 14.3g
- Cumin, 5.6g
- Smoked paprika, 5.6g
- Salt, 5.6g
- Chili powder, 2.8g
- Garlic powder, 2.8g
- Onion powder, 2.8g
- Black pepper, 1.4g
- Olive oil, 14ml
- Barbecue sauce, 14ml
- Hamburger buns, four

Coleslaw:
- Greek yogurt, 118ml
- Mayonnaise, 14ml
- Apple cider vinegar, 7ml
- Honey, 7ml
- Paprika, 1.4g
- Salt, 1.4g
- Black pepper, 1.4g
- Green cabbage, 128g, ¼-inch shreds
- Red cabbage, 128g, ¼-inch shreds
- Carrots, 64g, grated

Preparations:

Grilled Chicken:
1. Add chicken pieces into the plastic bag. Cut in half to make cutlets.
2. Mix the black pepper, onion powder, garlic powder, chili powder, salt, paprika, cumin, sugar, and brown into the bowl. Sprinkle the dry rub over each piece of chicken.
3. Insert grill plate in the cooking pot of Ninja foodi MAX health grill and air fryer and lock the lid. Choose the "grill" option.
4. Adjust the temperature to 175 degrees C. Adjust the cooking time to three to four minutes. Press the start/stop button to start preheating.
5. Place chicken onto the grill plate and lock the lid.
6. Open the lid and flip the pieces and cook for three to four minutes.
7. When done, remove from the grill.

Coleslaw:
1. Mix the pepper, salt, paprika, honey, apple cider vinegar, mayonnaise, and yogurt into the bowl.
2. Mix the carrots, red cabbage, and green cabbage into the big bowl.
3. Add dressing and toss to coat. Sprinkle with pepper and salt.
4. Toast the buns and place pulled chicken between the toasted buns.
5. Top with coleslaw and serve!

Nutrition:

CALORIES: 301KCAL, PROTEIN: 44G, CARBOHYDRATE: 20G, FAT: 6G

CRUMBED CHICKEN TENDERLOINS

 **PREPARATION TIME**
15 MINUTES

 **COOKING TIME**
12 MINUTES

 **SERVINGS**
4 PERSONS

Ingredients:

- Egg, one
- Dry breadcrumbs, 64g
- Vegetable oil, 29ml
- Chicken tenderloins, 1lb

Preparations:

1. Whisk the egg into the bowl. Combine the oil and breadcrumbs in another bowl.
2. Immerse chicken tenderloin into the egg and then crumb mixture.
3. Place coated chicken tenderloin into the air fryer basket.
4. Insert air fryer basket in the cooking pot of Ninja foodi MAX health grill and air fryer and lock the lid. Choose the "air fry" option.
5. Adjust the temperature to 160 degrees C. Adjust the cooking time to twelve minutes. Press the start/stop button to start preheating.
6. When done, remove and serve!

Nutrition:

CALORIES: 253KCAL, PROTEIN: 26.2G, CARBOHYDRATE: 9.8G, FAT: 11.4G

CHICKEN SPIEDINI WITH AMOGIO SAUCE

PREPARATION TIME
15 MINUTES

COOKING TIME
10 MINUTES

SERVINGS
4 PERSONS

Ingredients:

For the chicken skewers:
- Chicken breasts, 2lbs, cut into 1-inch cubes
- Olive oil, 78ml
- White wine, 59ml
- Rosemary, 28.3g, chopped
- Dried oregano, 14.3g
- Zest of lemon, one
- Salt, 5.6g
- Pepper, 5.6g
- Breadcrumbs, 96g
- Parmesan cheese, 43g, grated

For the amogio sauce:
- Olive oil, 118ml
- Butter, 59ml
- Garlic, three cloves, mince
- Lemon juice, 59ml
- Parsley, 14.3g, chopped
- Basil, 14.3g, chopped
- Salt, 1.4g
- Pepper, 1.4g
- Pinch red pepper flakes

Preparations:

1. Add pepper, salt, lemon zest, oregano, rosemary, wine, olive oil, and chicken into the bowl and toss to combine.
2. Place it into the refrigerator for twenty to thirty minutes.
3. Once marinated, toss in parmesan cheese and breadcrumbs.
4. Then, thread the chicken onto the skewers and keep it aside.
5. Insert roasting pan in the cooking pot of Ninja foodi MAX health grill and air fryer and lock the lid. Choose the "roast" option.
6. Adjust the temperature to 175 degrees C.
7. Adjust the cooking time to four minutes. Press the start/stop button to start preheating.
8. When done, remove from the grill.
9. Add amogio sauce ingredients into the saucepan and simmer it.
10. When done, pour over the chicken.

Nutrition:

CALORIES: 820KCAL, PROTEIN: 52G, CARBOHYDRATE: 4G, FAT: 65G

GRILLED CHICKEN WITH STRAWBERRY SALSA

 **PREPARATION TIME**
10 MINUTES

 **COOKING TIME**
20 MINUTES

 **SERVINGS**
4 PERSONS

Ingredients:

Strawberry salsa:
- Strawberries, 1lb, chopped
- Jalapeno peppers, two, ribs and seeds discard, chopped
- Onion, 32g, chopped
- Coriander, 32g, chopped
- Maple syrup, 7ml
- Juice of lime, one
- Pepper and salt, to taste

Chicken:
- Salt, 2.8g
- Pepper, 1.4g
- Cumin, 2.8g
- Chili powder, 5.6g
- Onion powder, 2.8g
- Garlic powder, 1.4g
- Olive oil, 29ml
- Chicken breasts, 2-3lbs

Preparations:

1. Combine strawberry salsa ingredients into the bowl.
2. Mix the garlic powder, onion powder, chili powder, cumin, pepper, and salt into the small dish.
3. Drizzle olive oil over the chicken breast. Rub seasoning mixture over the chicken breast.
4. Insert grill plate in the cooking pot of Ninja foodi MAX health grill and air fryer and lock the lid. Choose the "grill" option.
5. Adjust the temperature to 175 degrees C. Adjust the cooking time to fifteen to twenty minutes. Press the start/stop button to start preheating. Place grilled chicken onto the grill plate.
6. When done, remove from the grill.
7. Top with strawberry salsa.

Nutrition:

CALORIES: 377KCAL, PROTEIN: 49G, CARBOHYDRATE: 14G, FAT: 13G

VEGETABLES

TASTY GRILLED LEEKS

 **PREPARATION TIME**
20 MINUTES

 **COOKING TIME**
20 MINUTES

 **SERVINGS**
4 PERSONS

Ingredients:

- Salt, to taste
- Leeks, four, green tops removed, split in half, rinsed
- Extra-olive oil, 29ml
- Ground black pepper, to taste

Preparations:

1. Add ice water and salt into the pot and bring to boil.
2. Add leeks and boil for three to five minutes.
3. Transfer leeks to the ice water. Transfer it to the plate lined with a paper towel.
4. Insert grill plate in the cooking pot of Ninja foodi MAX health grill and air fryer and lock the lid. Choose the "grill" option.
5. Adjust the temperature to 160 degrees C. Adjust the cooking time to ten minutes. Press the start/stop button to start preheating.
6. Place leeks onto the grill plate and brush with oil.
7. When done, remove from the grill.
8. Season with pepper and salt.

Nutrition:

CALORIES: 69KCAL, PROTEIN: 2G, CARBOHYDRATE: 7G, FAT: 4G

GRILL-ROASTED CARROTS WITH SWEET SOY GLAZE

 **PREPARATION TIME**
10 MINUTES

 **COOKING TIME**
50 MINUTES

 SERVINGS
4 PERSONS

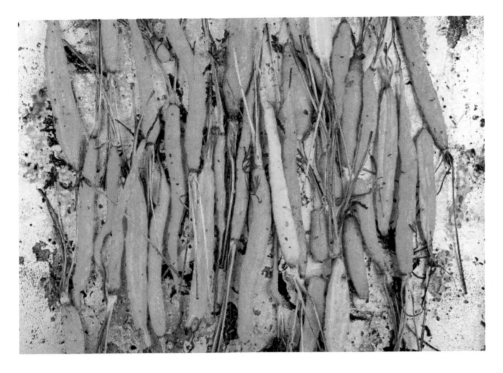

Ingredients:

- Honey, 59ml
- Soy sauce, 59ml
- Dark brown sugar, 14.3g
- Garlic, 5.6g, minced
- Fresh ginger, 2.8g, grated
- Red pepper flakes, 1.4g, crushed

For the carrots:
- Carrots, three, peeled and cut into ¾-inch slices
- Extra-virgin olive oil, 29ml
- Scallion, one, thinly sliced
- Salt, to taste

Preparations:

To prepare the glaze:
1. Whisk the crushed red pepper, ginger, garlic, brown sugar, soy sauce, and honey into the bowl. Keep it aside.

To prepare the carrots:
1. Toss carrot slices with oil into the medium bowl. Sprinkle with salt.
2. Insert grill plate in the cooking pot of Ninja foodi MAX health grill and air fryer and lock the lid. Choose the "grill" option.
3. Adjust the temperature to 175 degrees C. Adjust the cooking time to forty-five minutes. Press the start/stop button to start preheating.
4. Place carrot onto the grill plate and brush with oil.
5. Flip every fifteen minutes. Brush with glaze and again lock the lid. Cook for three minutes more.
6. Garnish with scallions.

Nutrition:

CALORIES: 106KCAL, PROTEIN: 2G, CARBOHYDRATE: 16G, FAT: 5G

GRILLED CABBAGE WITH BLUE CHEESE DRESSING

 PREPARATION TIME
10 MINUTES

 COOKING TIME
30 MINUTES

 SERVINGS
4-6 PERSONS

Ingredients:

- Crumbled blue cheese, 0.25lb
- Mayonnaise, 118ml
- Sour cream, 118ml
- Juice of lemon, 14ml
- Salt and ground black pepper, to taste
- Head green cabbage, one, cut into six wedges
- Extra-virgin olive oil, 29ml
- Scallions, 32g, sliced
- Cherry tomatoes, 128g, split in half
- Bacon, 64g, cooked and crumbled

Preparations:

1. Add blue cheese into the bowl and mash it using a fork.
2. Then, add lemon juice, sour cream, and mayonnaise and whisk to combine. Sprinkle with pepper and salt. Coat the cabbage with this mixture and top with cheese.
3. Insert grill plate in the cooking pot of Ninja foodi MAX health grill and air fryer and lock the lid. Choose the "grill" option.
4. Adjust the temperature to 160 degrees C. Adjust the cooking time to ten minutes. Press the start/stop button to start preheating.
5. Place cabbage wedges onto the grill plate. Lock the lid.
6. Flip cabbage after five minutes and cook for five minutes more.
7. When done, transfer cabbage into the bowl. Toss with pepper, olive oil, and salt. Top with bacon.
8. Serve and enjoy!

Nutrition:

CALORIES: 98KCAL, PROTEIN: 2G, CARBOHYDRATE: 7G, FAT: 8G

HALLOUMI AND VEGETABLE SKEWERS

 **PREPARATION TIME**
10 MINUTES

 COOKING TIME
20 MINUTES

 SERVINGS
6-8 PERSONS

Ingredients:

- Olive oil, 59ml
- Lemon juice, 29ml
- Red wine vinegar, 29ml
- Garlic, 10g, minced
- Dried oregano, 10g
- Mint leaves, 5.6g, chopped
- Salt and ground black pepper, to taste
- Halloumi cheese, 1lb, cut into 3/4-inch cubes
- Zucchini, two, cut into 1/2-inch rounds
- Red onions, two, peeled and cut into ¾-inch chunks
- Grape tomatoes, one pint

Preparations:

1. Whisk the mint, oregano, garlic, vinegar, oil, and lemon juice into the bowl. Sprinkle with pepper and salt.
2. Add tomatoes, onion, zucchini, and cheese and toss to combine.
3. Thread tomatoes, onion, zucchini, and cheese onto the skewers.
4. Insert roasting pan in the cooking pot of Ninja foodi MAX health grill and air fryer and lock the lid. Choose the "roast" option.
5. Adjust the temperature to 175 degrees C. Adjust the cooking time to ten minutes. Press the start/stop button to start preheating.
6. Place skewers onto the roasting pan. Lock the lid.
7. When done, squeeze lemon wedges over it.

Nutrition:

CALORIES: 165KCAL, PROTEIN: 11.6G, CARBOHYDRATE: 4.6G, FAT: 11G

GRILLED SKEWERED SHISHITO PEPPERS

 **PREPARATION TIME**
5 MINUTES

 **COOKING TIME**
15 MINUTES

 **SERVINGS**
4 PERSONS

Ingredients:

- Shishito peppers, 1lb
- Salt and ground black pepper, to taste
- Teriyaki sauce, 59ml

Preparations:

1. Firstly, thread shishito peppers onto the skewers. Season with pepper and salt.
2. Insert grill plate in the cooking pot of Ninja foodi MAX health grill and air fryer and lock the lid. Choose the "grill" option.
3. Adjust the temperature to 180 degrees C. Adjust the cooking time to five minutes. Press the start/stop button to start preheating.
4. Place shishito peppers onto the grill.
5. When done, remove from the grill.
6. Top with teriyaki sauce.

Nutrition:

CALORIES: 96KCAL, PROTEIN:1G, CARBOHYDRATE: 9G, FAT: 1G

GRILLED SUMMER SQUASH WITH CHIMICHURRI

 **PREPARATION TIME**
10 MINUTES

 COOKING TIME
15 MINUTES

 SERVINGS
4-6 PERSONS

Ingredients:

- Yellow onion, 64g, chopped
- Garlic, 5.6g, minced
- Jalapeno, 28.3g, minced, stemmed and seeded
- Red wine vinegar, 118ml
- Parsley leaves, 96g, chopped
- Cilantro leaves, 32g, chopped
- Extra-virgin olive oil, 236ml
- Ground black pepper and sea salt, to taste
- Zucchini, two, end trimmed and halved
- Yellow summer squash, two, end trimmed and halved

Preparations:

1. Mix the red wine vinegar, jalapeno, garlic, and onion into the bowl.
2. Let rest for ten minutes. Add olive oil, cilantro, and fresh parsley leaves. Season with pepper and salt. Let stand chimichurri for one hour. Season zucchini and squash with pepper and black salt. Brush with oil.
3. Insert grill plate in the cooking pot of Ninja foodi MAX health grill and air fryer and lock the lid. Choose the "grill" option.
4. Adjust the temperature to 180 degrees C. Adjust the cooking time to ten minutes. Press the start/stop button to start preheating.
5. Place vegetables onto the grill plate.
6. When done, place onto the plate and top with chimichurri sauce over it.

Nutrition:

CALORIES: 53KCAL, PROTEIN:2G, CARBOHYDRATE: 7G, FAT: 2G

GRILLED RAMPS

 **PREPARATION TIME**
5 MINUTES

 **COOKING TIME**
5 MINUTES

 **SERVINGS**
4 PERSONS

Ingredients:

- Ramps, thirty-two, cleaned and trimmed
- Extra virgin olive oil, 29ml
- Salt and ground black pepper, to taste

Preparations:

1. Place ramps onto the plate and drizzle with olive oil, and sprinkle with pepper and salt. Toss to combine.
2. Insert grill plate in the cooking pot of Ninja foodi MAX health grill and air fryer and lock the lid. Choose the "grill" option.
3. Adjust the temperature to 180 degrees C. Adjust the cooking time to five minutes. Press the start/stop button to start preheating.
4. Place ramps onto the grill plate.
5. When done, remove and serve!

Nutrition:

CALORIES: 34KCAL, PROTEIN: 2G, CARBOHYDRATE: 1G, FIBER: 1G

GRILLED ROMAINE HEARTS WITH BUTTERMILK-DILL DRESSING

PREPARATION TIME
5 MINUTES

COOKING TIME
15 MINUTES

SERVINGS
6 PERSONS

Ingredients:

- Extra-virgin olive oil, 44ml
- Salt and ground black pepper, to taste
- Lettuce hearts, three, core intact, halved lengthwise
- Dijon mustard, 14ml
- Mayonnaise, 29ml
- Apple cider vinegar, 29ml
- Shallot, half, peeled and minced
- Sugar, 14.3g
- Fresh dill, 42g, chopped
- Grape tomatoes, half pint, halved lengthwise
- Radishes, four, thinly sliced

Preparations:

1. Mix the pepper, salt, and oil into the bowl. Brush on each lettuce with half of the oil mixture. Keep it aside.
2. Mix the pepper, salt, dill, sugar, shallot, vinegar, mayonnaise, and mustard into the Mason jar and keep it aside.
3. Insert grill plate in the cooking pot of Ninja foodi MAX health grill and air fryer and lock the lid. Choose the "grill" option.
4. Adjust the temperature to 160 degrees C. Adjust the cooking time to seven minutes. Press the start/stop button to start preheating.
5. Place lettuce leaves onto the grill plate.
6. When done, place onto the plate and top with dressing.
7. Garnish with sliced radishes and tomatoes.

Nutrition:

CALORIES: 88KCAL, PROTEIN: 1.9G, CARBOHYDRATE: 4.2G, FAT: 7.5G

GRILLED BUTTERNUT SQUASH

 **PREPARATION TIME**
10 MINUTES

 COOKING TIME
30 MINUTES

 SERVINGS
4 PERSONS

Ingredients:

- Pine nuts, 28.3g
- Butternut squash, one, peeled, seeded, and cut into 1-inch cubes
- Extra-virgin olive oil, 29ml
- Fresh cheese, 226g
- Sage, 14.3g, chopped
- Salt and ground black pepper, to taste

Preparations:

1. Add pine nuts into the skillet and cook over medium-high flame. Let toast it until browned. Transfer it to the bowl. Keep it aside.
2. Add squash into the bowl and toss with pepper and salt.
3. Insert grill plate in the cooking pot of Ninja foodi MAX health grill and air fryer and lock the lid. Choose the "grill" option.
4. Adjust the temperature to 180 degrees C. Adjust the cooking time to thirty minutes. Press the start/stop button to start preheating.
5. Place tossed squash onto the grill plate.
6. When done, transfer it to the plate.
7. Top with sage, pine nuts, and ricotta. Season with pepper and salt.

Nutrition:

CALORIES: 100KCAL, PROTEIN: 2G, CARBOHYDRATE: 23.9G, FAT: 1.2G

GRILLED BRUSSELS SPROUTS

PREPARATION TIME
10 MINUTES

COOKING TIME
13 MINUTES

SERVINGS
4 PERSONS

Ingredients:

- Brussels sprouts, 1lb
- Olive oil, 29ml
- Garlic, 14.3g, minced
- Mustard, 5ml
- Smoked paprika, 5.6g
- Salt, 5.6g
- Ground black pepper, 1.4g

Preparations:

1. Cut off the stem of the Brussels sprouts and remove yellowing leaves.
2. Add Brussels sprouts into the microwave bowl and microwave it for three minutes at high temperature.
3. Add salt, paprika, mustard, garlic, and olive oil and toss to combine. Let cool it. Thread Brussels sprouts onto the skewers.
4. Insert grill plate in the cooking pot of Ninja foodi MAX health grill and air fryer and lock the lid. Choose the "grill" option.
5. Adjust the temperature to 180 degrees C. Adjust the cooking time to ten minutes. Press the start/stop button to start preheating.
6. Place skewers onto the grill plate.
7. When done, remove from the grill.
8. Place back to the mixing bowl and toss with oil and garlic mixture.

Nutrition:

CALORIES: 55KCAL, PROTEIN: 2.1G, CARBOHYDRATE: 6.4G, FAT: 3.1G

CONCLUSION

I wholeheartedly thank you and give you my warmest regards and appreciation for finding this book interesting enough to have read it all through to the end. I sincerely hope that you found the information and recipes found inside this book to be fruitful and that they helped you in your culinary journey.

Ninja Kitchen has been dishing out some of the most innovative and accessible cooking appliances right now in the market designed to make the lives of both novice and master chefs easier while making the cooking experience a breeze. The Smart Ninja Grill XL isn't an exception, and this fully holds up to the legacy and expectation set by the appliances that came before.

Grilling and BBQ-ing is a hobby that deep down everybody wants to pursue, and eve-rybody enjoys it. However, the lack of skills, manpower, environment, and various other factors such as location, weather, and so on often stand as a hurdle when firing up an outdoor charcoal grill for a backyard party.

Under such circumstances, the Ninja Grill Smart XL truly came as a revolutionary piece of cooking equipment that allowed you to Grill, Air Crisp/Air Fry meals, Bake, Roast, and even Broil your meals with absolute ease!

While the recipe book included with the appliance itself is aright, the limited number of recipes and information regarding the appliance can seem like a hurdle to absolute begin-ners.

This book was written to be a very user-friendly and easily accessible Ninja Grill Smart XL companion book that would make learning the basics of the appliance much easier and friendly.

Upon understanding the book's fundamentals, the wide variety of 500 recipes careful-ly separated over 9 different chapters and grouped according to ingredients are present-ed in a way that anyone can pick up, find what they are looking for and start cooking right away!

The recipes themselves range from absolute beginner level ones to even some hard ones, so no matter your skill level, you are bound to find something that you will enjoy.

The provided cooking charts and conversion tables are also prepared to help you need a quick lookup. Have a look at the cookbook that comes with your appliance and that one has an even more in-depth cooking time chart.

In the end, I would like to say that I completely realize that no one book can be abso-lutely perfect and cannot hold all of the information in the world; however, I still tried my very best to produce a scripture that would give value to my readers and help them mas-ter their newly bought Ninja Smart XL Grill.

With that said, if this book helped you in any way or if you were able to find a recipe that you like, please be kind enough to take some time and leave a review for me. Your inspiring reviews will encourage me further to produce more books such as these for my readers.

Thank you, and stay safe.

God Bless.

INDEX

Printed in Great Britain
by Amazon